FML

Quick and Easy Crafts

Greetings Cards

15 step-by-step projects – simple to make, stunning results

CHERYL OWEN

NEW HOLLAND

Published in 2004 by
New Holland Publishers (UK) Ltd
London • Cape Town • Sydney • Auckland
www.newhollandpublishers.com

Garfield House, 86–88 Edgware Road, London W2 2EA, United Kingdom

80 McKenzie Street, Cape Town 8001, South Africa

14 Aquatic Drive, Frenchs Forest, NSW 2086, Australia

218 Lake Road, Northcote, Auckland, New Zealand

ISBN 1 84330 694 8

Senior Editor: Clare Hubbard
Production: Hazel Kirkman
Design: AG&G Books, Glyn Bridgewater
Photographer: Shona Wood
Templates: Steve Dew
Editorial Direction: Rosemary Wilkinson

10 9 8 7 6 5 4 3 2 1

Reproduction by Pica Digital Ltd, Singapore
Printed and bound by Times Offset, Malaysia

Disclaimer
The author and publishers have made every effort to ensure that all
instructions given in this book are safe and accurate, but they cannot accept
liability for any resulting injuries or loss or damage to either property or
person, whether direct or consequential and howsoever arising.

Contents

 # Projects

Introduction

Giving a hand-crafted greetings card shows the recipient just how much you care about them and this book presents masses of innovative ideas for all sorts of special occasions. In the projects the most popular card-making techniques are explored and they provide a great opportunity to try out new materials. Making the greetings cards in this book does not require much time and only the most basic of equipment.

There are projects for the beginner and the experienced card maker, and with so many special days to mark throughout the year you'll never run out of reasons to be creative. It is surprising how quickly many of the cards can be made; which is great for when you want to produce multiples – for invitations or Christmas cards for example. On the other hand, a red letter day can be highlighted with a one-off creation to be treasured. For that extra personal touch, there are instructions to show how your cards can be delivered in beautifully hand-crafted envelopes.

Each project is accompanied by concise instructions and step-by-step photographs. Easy-to-use templates that will ensure a professional finish can be found on pages 74–77. Once you have mastered techniques that are new to you, start to be inventive and have fun creating your own wonderful designs.

 Tools

For safety and best results, work on a well-lit, clean, flat surface and take care to keep all of your tools in a safe place, away from children and pets.

Drawing

An HB pencil is the most useful for drawing. A softer pencil, such as a 2B, is recommended for transferring images. For accuracy, keep pencils sharpened to a point or use a propelling pencil. Use a ruler and set square to draw squares and rectangles accurately.

Cutting

A craft knife or scalpel is indispensible for cutting straight lines. Craft knives are better than scissors for cutting card because the card is kept flat while cutting. Rest on a self-healing cutting mat when using a craft knife or scalpel, cutting straight edges against a metal ruler. Change the blades often as a blunt blade will tear the surface of paper and card. Always take care when handling the blades. A craft knife can also be used to score card so that it folds neatly. A bone folder, which is a traditional bookbinding tool, is best for scoring though, and worth getting if you intend to make a lot of greetings cards. It will also be useful for other paper crafts.

Choose scissors that are comfortable to handle; a sharp pair of general scissors are the most versatile. Small, intricate shapes can be cut with embroidery scissors. Pinking shears and fancy-edge scissors cut with a shaped edge and

give a decorative touch to projects. Paper punches come in all sorts of shapes and can be used to punch decorative holes in paper.

Pierce small holes with a pin or use a bradawl on a cutting mat for larger holes. A hole punch makes a neat hole quickly. Use wire cutters or an old pair of scissors to cut wire.

Painting

A few good quality artist's paintbrushes such as a round brush, a flat brush and a couple of stencil brushes are the most versatile for painting greetings cards. Expand the range if you intend to paint a lot of

cards. Always clean brushes immediately after use.

Stretch silk for painting on a silk frame or improvise with an embroidery frame. Attach the silk to the frame with three-prong silk pins as they will not mark the silk.

Safety

When using any tools or materials always follow the manufacturer's instructions carefully.

Materials

Paper and card

There is a superb choice of paper and card widely available nowadays. Art shops and specialist paper shops have globally sourced colourful papers. Look out for handmade papers incorporating petals, leaves, seeds or metallic fragments, embossed with patterns and textured with fibres. Although handmade papers are often expensive, a single sheet will make many greetings cards. Translucent papers will subtly display the colours underneath them. There are also decorative papers that have glamorous surface embellishments such as embroidery or glitter. Create your own by stitching on paper with shiny thread or applying glitter with relief pens. High-quality stationers sell single sheets of writing paper in lots of colours and this is often an economic way of buying a small amount of paper with envelopes to match.

Card comes in lots of different finishes, such as metallic and pearlized. Cut stencils from stencil sheets that have an oiled surface that prevents paint seeping through. Corrugated card is inexpensive and comes in a range of colourways to match a project.

Mixed media

Decorate your greetings cards with various craft materials. Emboss fine metal with simple images. Wire is available in different thicknesses and lovely colours from jewellery-making suppliers. Use a pair of jewellery pliers to manipulate the wire. There is a wide range of rubber stamps available and inkpads in lots of shades; they are a fast way to achieve a professional finish.

Sticking

Read the manufacturer's instructions and test adhesives on spare paper before use. PVA (white) glue is a very versatile, non-toxic adhesive. It will stick paper, card, fabric and wood. All-purpose household glue is surprisingly strong and will stick many materials. It is best for gluing small areas, as it does not spread evenly over a large surface. Spread glue with a plastic glue spreader. Alternatively, improvise and spread glue with a scrap of card. Use spray adhesive to stick layers of paper and card. Double-sided tape is a clean, neat way to join paper and card. Use adhesive foam to stick motifs so they sit proud of the card. Use low-tack masking tape to stick templates and work temporarily, but check first that it will not tear or mark the work.

Painting

Always use the correct paint for the job. Test paints on spare paper and card first, as some paints will warp them. Acrylic paints can be mixed easily and will dry quickly.

Glass paints give a luxurious, transparent colour on acetate. They come in a large range of colours and can be mixed. Apply glass outliner to acetate first to create different areas then flood the areas, with the glass paints. Use silk paints on silk material. These are water-based paints applied in a similar way to glass paints in that areas are drawn on stretched silk with silk outliner (gutta) and paint is then flooded in to fill the outlined shapes.

Relief paints in pearlized and glitter finishes are simple and fun to use. Designs painted with masking fluid can be painted over then rubbed away to reveal the paper underneath.

Decoration

It is often the small embellishments that make a greetings card special. For glamour add beads, sequins and cabochon jewellery stones and finish with silky cords and tassels.

Unexpected everyday items can also be incorporated; save foil sweet wrappers, buttons and scraps of ribbon and lace for use on your cards. Colourful pieces of wallpaper and gift-wrap are ideal for making greetings cards.

Nature also provides a host of decorations. Press flowers and leaves from the garden and collect tiny shells, pebbles and feathers when out walking.

If adding three-dimensional elements, consider how you will pack the cards, especially if they are to be sent through the post. A padded envelope will give protection and a hand delivered card can have a box envelope. Decorate envelopes that will be delivered by hand to co-ordinate with the greetings card.

Materials are shown on page 10.

Materials. See page 9 for descriptions.

Techniques

The same basic techniques occur throughout the projects. Always read the instructions for a project before embarking upon it and try out new techniques on scrap paper first. Use metric or imperial measurements but not a combination of both.

Using templates

Trace the image onto tracing paper, drawing straight lines against a ruler. Turn the tracing over and redraw it on the wrong side with a soft pencil. Use masking tape to tape the tracing right side up on your chosen paper or card. Redraw the design to transfer it using a sharp HB pencil. If you wish to use the template more than once or twice, transfer it onto thin card to cut out and draw around.

Enlarging and reducing templates on a photocopier

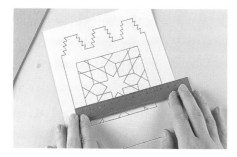

For speed and accuracy use a photocopier to enlarge or reduce a motif. You will need to calculate your enlargement percentage. Firstly you need to know what width you want the final image to be. Then measure the width of the original motif that you want to photocopy. Divide the first measurement by the second and then multiply the answer by 100 to find the percentage by which you need to enlarge the motif. For example, a motif needs to be enlarged to 150 mm and the original width is 120 mm. Using the calculation you can work out that, 150 divided by 120 and then mutliplied by 100 makes the percentage increase 125%. Remember that an enlargement must always be more than 100% and a reduction less than 100%.

Enlarging and reducing templates on a grid

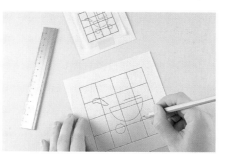

To enlarge or reduce a motif by hand on a grid, tape a piece of tracing paper over the original design with masking tape. Draw a square or rectangle on top, enclosing the image and divide it up with a row of vertical and horizontal lines. The spacing will depend upon the size and intricacy of the design. Complex designs should have lines about 1 cm ($3/8$ in) apart and simpler ones 2.5 cm (1 in) apart.

Draw a square or rectangle of the required finished size to the same proportions as the square or rectangle on the tracing paper. Divide into the same number of vertical and horizontal lines. Redraw the image working on one square or rectangle at a time, then view the design as a whole and redraw any areas that do not seem to "flow" well.

Using a craft knife

Cut straight edges on paper and card with a craft knife or scalpel against a metal ruler, resting on a cutting mat. When cutting card, do not press too hard or attempt to cut right through at the first approach, it is easier to gradually cut deeper and deeper.

Scoring

It is easier and neater to fold card if a fold line has been scored first. A bone folder, (a traditional book-binder's tool), is recommended for scoring; score with the pointed end against a ruler. Alternatively, lightly score with a craft knife taking care to break the top surface only.

Folding

A bone folder is useful for folding paper and card. Press the flat of the bone folder on the fold and run it smoothly along its length. If you do not have a bone folder, press your thumb along the fold to flatten it.

Using spray adhesive

Always use spray adhesive in a well-ventilated room and protect the surrounding area with newspaper. If sticking large pieces, smooth them out from the centre for an even finish.

Strengthening paper

Fine paper can be used for making greetings cards. To strengthen the paper, cut it approximately 1 cm

(½ in) larger all round than the finished size. Spray mount the paper to card, smoothing it outwards from the centre. Cut to the required size.

Creating a deckle edge

1 Place a ruler on the paper where you wish to tear it. Dip an artist's paintbrush in water and run it along the ruler's edge to soften the paper or card. If the card is very thick, you may need to repeat on the other side of the card too.

2 Holding the ruler firmly in position, tear the paper against it.

Making an insert

An insert gives a formal touch. It is useful to add a light coloured insert if the inside of the greetings card is dark in colour and therefore difficult to be written on clearly. Open the card out flat. Cut the insert paper 5 mm (¼ in) smaller than the card on all sides. Fold the insert in half. Run a line of paper glue close to the fold of the insert. Stick it inside the back of the greetings card, matching the folds.

Making a basic envelope

1 To make a template, measure the card front and draw it on scrap paper adding 5 mm (¼ in) to each edge. Draw the flap on the upper edge half the width of the front. Draw the back at the lower edge, 4 cm (1½ in) less than the width of the front. Draw a 2.5 cm (1 in) wide tab each side of the front. Draw a curve at each corner; a coin or button is a useful template for the curves.

2 Cut out the template and draw around it on paper or thin card. Score along the edges of the front

with a bone folder or lightly with a craft knife. Fold along the lines, folding the tabs under the back.

3 Open out the back again. Apply 1 cm ($^1/_2$ in) wide double-sided tape along the side edges of the inner back, starting 2.5 cm (1 in) below the upper edge. Peel off the backing tapes and stick the back over the tabs. Tuck the flap inside the back or seal it with double-sided tape.

Making a lined envelope

Choose thin paper or gift-wrap for the lining so the envelope folds neatly and is not too bulky and untidy.

Follow the Making a basic envelope, step 1. Cut the front and flap shape from the lining paper, trimming 5 mm ($^1/_4$ in) from the outer edges. Stick the lining to the inside of the envelope, 5 mm ($^1/_4$ in) inside the edges, with spray adhesive. Continue making up the envelope following the basic envelope steps 2 and 3.

Making a padded envelope

Present delicate greetings cards in a padded envelope for protection.

Measure the card front and draw it on scrap paper adding 1 cm ($^3/_8$ in) to each edge. Draw up the envelope referring to the Making a basic envelope instructions opposite. Cut out the envelope. Cut the front and back shape from bubble-wrap and stick to the inside of the envelope using spray adhesive, with the smooth side of the bubble-wrap uppermost. Apply 1 cm ($^1/_2$ in) wide double-sided tape along the side edges of the tabs on the inside, starting 5.5 cm ($2^1/_4$ in) below the upper edge. Fold the back over the front. Peel off the backing tapes and stick the tabs over the back. Seal the flap over the back with double-sided tape.

Making a box envelope

Present a hand-delivered greetings card in a custom-made box. For protection, line the box and lid with bubble wrap, fill the box with shredded tissue, or wrap the card in tissue paper.
1 Measure the card front and draw it on scrap paper, adding 5 mm ($^1/_4$ in) to each edge. This will be the base. Measure the depth of the card (take into account items that stand proud).

Draw a side to the base along each edge that is the depth of the card plus 5 mm ($^1/_4$ in). Add a 1.5 cm ($^3/_4$ in) wide tab to both ends of two opposite box sides and draw a slanted end to the tabs.

2 Cut out the template and use it to cut a box from card. Score along the lines with a bone folder or a craft knife. Fold the side edges upwards. Stick the tabs under the opposite ends of the sides with double-sided tape. Make a lid in the same way as the box but adding 2 mm ($^1/_{10}$ in) to each edge of the base.

Adapting craft techniques

If you have a favourite craft adapt it for making greetings cards by making it less time-consuming. Embroider simple motifs for example, or paint a series of characters that can be cut out and used separately. By experimenting you will find ways to simplify the technique without losing its appeal.

3D bird house

Send a charming bird house to the proud owner of a new home. The three-dimensional house folds flat to fit an envelope and a real twig attached to the front is a delightful finishing touch. The roof is made of vibrant corrugated card and the house itself is constructed from ridged card. Write your message on the underside of the roof.

Ordinary corrugated packaging card can be used for the roof. Simply paint it a bright colour.

You will need

Materials

- Tracing paper
- Masking tape
- A4 sheet of white ridged card
- Double-sided tape
- A5 sheet of red or blue corrugated card
- Small twig
- All-purpose household glue

Tools

- Soft pencil
- Cutting mat
- Craft knife
- Bone folder (optional)
- Metal ruler
- Scissors

1 Trace the bird house template on page 74 onto tracing paper with a soft pencil. Turn the tracing over and redraw it on the reverse. Tape the tracing right side up on white ridged card with masking tape. Redraw to transfer. Remove the tracing. Resting on a cutting mat, cut out the house and the hole with a craft knife.

2 Score the bird house along the broken lines using a bone folder or craft knife. Apply double-sided tape to the tabs on the right side. Fold the bird house along the scored lines with the inner sides facing to form the bird house shape.

★☆☆ **Skill level**   🕐 **2 hours**   **Techniques:** *Using templates p. 11, Using a craft knife p. 11, Scoring p. 11, Folding p.12*

3 Peel the backing tape off the house tab. Stick the tab under the opposite end of the bird house.

4 Trace the roof template on page 74 onto tracing paper with a soft pencil. Turn the paper over and redraw it on the reverse side. Transfer the roof template to red or blue corrugated card with the corrugations parallel with the short edges. Draw the tab position on the inside. Fold the roof in half then open out flat.

5 Peel the backing tape off the roof tab on the house. With the roof inside facing up, stick the house roof tab onto the tab position on the inside of the roof. Fold the other end of the roof over the top of the bird house.

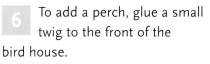

6 To add a perch, glue a small twig to the front of the bird house.

Helpful hint
Slip a piece of bubble-wrap into the envelope when sending this greetings card to protect the twig perch from damage.

Variation

Gingerbread house

This appetizing gingerbread house is made of brown card. It has been decorated with a white relief pen and left to dry before being constructed.

Anniversary image transfer

The treasured family photograph on this glamorous greetings card has been photocopied then embellished with glitter and cabochon jewellery stones. A silk border, flamboyant organza ribbon and beads add to its opulence. Add an insert to give the greeting extra importance.

Do not use heirloom photographs to make greetings cards. Photocopy your favourites so the originals can be kept safe and intact.

You will need

Materials

- Postcard-size photo
- Glitter relief paints
- Pink silk dupion (1.5 cm/ 3/4 in larger than photo)
- Spray adhesive
- A3 sheet of white card
- Selection of cabochon jewellery stones
- All-purpose household glue
- A3 sheet of cream paper
- Paper glue
- 90 cm (1 yd) of 1 cm (1/2 in) wide pink organza ribbon
- 8 small crystal beads with large holes
- 2 large pink beads with large holes

Tools

- Craft knife
- Metal ruler
- Cutting mat
- Fabric scissors
- Bone folder (optional)
- Tweezers (optional)
- Large-eyed needle

1 Photocopy your photograph and cut it out, trimming it to a different size if you wish. Highlight details on the photo using glitter relief paints.

2 Cut a rectangle of pink silk 1.5 cm (3/4 in) larger on all sides than the photocopy. Stick the photocopy onto the silk with spray adhesive.

★★☆ **Skill level**   🕐 **2 hours**   **Techniques:** *Scoring p. 11, Folding p. 12, Using spray adhesive p. 12, Making an insert p. 12*

3 Cut a rectangle of white card 33 x 20.5 cm (13 x 8 in). Score across the centre parallel with the short edges. Fold the card in half along the scored line. Stick the image to the front with spray adhesive. Glue a cabochon jewellery stone at each corner with all-purpose household glue. Use tweezers to position them if you find it easier.

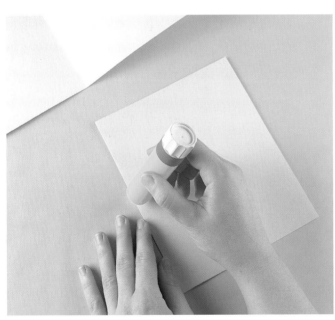

4 Cut a rectangle of cream paper 32 x 19.5 cm (12³/₄ x 7³/₄ in) to use as an insert. Fold the insert in half, parallel with the short edges. Run a line of paper glue close to the fold of the insert and stick it inside the back of the greetings card, matching the folds.

5 Fold the ribbon in half and slip it inside the card between the pages of the insert with the fold at the top. Close the card and bring the ends of the ribbon up over the front of the card and through the loop at the top.

6 Thread a needle on one ribbon end, slip three crystal beads, one pink bead and another crystal bead on the ribbon. Knot the ribbon under the beads. Repeat on the other end. Carefully cut off the excess ribbon.

Helpful hint

If you do not have a needle with an eye large enough for the ribbon, bend fine wire in half and slip the ribbon through the fold and use it as a needle. Alternatively you could use a bodkin.

Variation

White silk

This elegant photocopy has been applied to white silk with a frayed edge. A few simple embroidery stitches worked in gold thread add understated decoration.

Beaded heart concertina

A concertina greetings card provides lots of space to write long messages or even stick in photographs. Its pages open in folds and both sides can be written on. The cover is decorated with a bold heart worked from beads threaded onto wire.

The heart is an ideal motif for a Valentine card and the concertina pages allow a lengthy, heartfelt message to be written.

You will need

Materials

- 1 mm (1/24 in) diameter wire
- Assorted pink beads
- A4 sheet of thick white card
- A3 sheet of purple paper
- PVA glue
- Matching thread
- A2 sheet of thick red paper

Tools

- Wire cutters or an old pair of scissors
- Jeweller's pliers
- Craft knife
- Metal ruler
- Cutting mat
- Glue spreader
- Needle
- Scissors
- Bone folder (optional)

1 Snip a 29 cm (11½ in) length of wire. Bend 2.5 cm (1 in) at one end at a right angle to stop the beads slipping off. Thread assorted pink beads onto the wire stopping 2.5 cm (1 in) from the end.

Helpful hint
Always snip wire with wire cutters or an old pair of scissors as the wire will blunt a sharp pair.

★★☆ **Skill level**   🕐 **3 hours**   **Techniques:** *Using a craft knife p.11, Scoring p.11, Folding p.12*

2 Link the ends of the wire together with a pair of jeweller's pliers, forming a ring. Bend the ring into a heart shape making sure the join forms the bottom point. Snip off the excess wire.

3 Resting on a cutting mat, use a craft knife to cut two 11.5 cm (4½ in) squares of thick white card and two 15.5 cm (6 in) squares of purple paper for the front and back of the card. Place the card squares centrally on the reverse side of the papers. Glue the corners, then the edges of the paper over the card.

4 Place the heart on the front. Pierce two holes with the needle, one either side of the top point of the heart. Thread the needle with thread, push it up through one hole from the reverse side and down through the other hole capturing the heart against the front. Tie the thread ends securely on the reverse side.

5 Cut a 55 cm (21¼ in) long strip of 11.5 cm (4½ in) wide red paper for the pages. Score the pages with a bone folder or lightly with a craft knife. Fold in concertina folds 11 cm (4¼ in) wide.

6 Spread glue evenly on the back page with a glue spreader. Stick the pages centrally to the reverse side of the back cover. Spread glue on the front page and press the front cover on top, lining it up with the back cover.

Variation

Bead spiral

A spiral is very simple to model from beads threaded onto wire. This concertina card of vibrant blue beads on a bright green background has pages to match the beads.

Embossed metal fern

Subtle effects are achieved by embossing designs on fine metal, which is available in sheet form from craft shops. This handsome fern is set off by the metal stud fastening. An insert of matching translucent paper lends a formal tone to this greetings card.

Metal studs are easy to apply. They come in lots of different shapes and are available from haberdashery departments.

You will need

Materials

- Tracing paper
- A4 sheet of fine pewter metal
- Masking tape
- Kitchen towel
- A3 sheet of bright green card
- 3 round metal studs
- A3 sheet of bright green translucent paper
- All-purpose household glue

Tools

- Pen
- Metal cutters or an old pair of scissors
- Scissors
- Ballpoint pen
- Cutting mat
- Craft knife
- Metal ruler
- Bone folder (optional)
- Bradawl

1 Trace the fern template on page 75 onto tracing paper with a pen. With a pair of metal cutters or an old pair of scissors, cut a 20.5 x 13.5 cm (8 x 5¼ in) rectangle of fine pewter metal. Tape the tracing right side up on top with masking tape.

2 Place the metal and tracing on two sheets of kitchen towel. To emboss the design, trace the ferns with a ballpoint pen. Remove the tracing.

★★☆ **Skill level**   🕐 **2 hours**   **Techniques:** *Using templates p.11, Using a craft knife p.11, Scoring, p.11, Using spray adhesive p. 12*

3 Resting on a cutting mat, use a craft knife to cut two 23.5 x 19.5 cm (9¼ x 7¾ in) rectangles of bright green card for the front and back. Using a bone folder or craft knife, score across the front 3 cm (1¼ in) in from the left-hand edge to create a hinge.

Helpful hint
If you have one to hand a specialist embossing tool can be used to emboss the metal, rather than a ballpoint pen.

4 Place a stud in the centre of the hinge. Press the stud to make indentations with the prongs. Position the remaining studs 1.5 cm (¾ in) from the upper and lower edges. Indent the hinge with the prongs as before to mark the positions of the studs.

5 Resting on a cutting mat, use a craft knife to cut two 22.5 x 19 cm (9 x 7½ in) rectangles of green translucent paper for the inserts. Place the back of the card on the cutting mat, position the inserts on top with the left edges level and the card extending 5 mm (⅛ in) above and below the inserts. Place the front on top.

6 Use a bradawl to enlarge the prong holes and pierce them through to the back page.

7 Starting at the centre holes, insert the prongs of a stud through the holes and close them over the back card to secure all the layers together. Fix the other studs in the same way. Glue the fern to the front.

Resist-painted Easter egg

Welcome springtime with a colourful, jaunty Easter egg. The vibrant colours on this greetings card are painted over patterns created with masking fluid which is then rubbed away when the paint has dried to reveal the paper underneath.

To make the motifs stand proud of the card, fix them in place with pieces of adhesive foam.

You will need

Materials

- A3 sheet of watercolour paper
- Masking fluid
- Tracing paper
- Masking tape
- Scrap paper
- Pink, lilac, light blue and yellow acrylic paints
- Adhesive foam

Tools

- Craft knife
- Metal ruler
- Cutting mat
- Artist's paintbrush
- Soft pencil
- Scissors
- Flat 2 cm (¾ in) paintbrush
- Bone folder (optional)
- Fancy-edged scissors

1 Cut a 25 x 18 cm (10 x 7 in) rectangle of watercolour paper. With an artist's paintbrush, apply spots of masking fluid to the paper at random and then leave to dry.

2 With a soft pencil, draw a strip 11 x 3 cm (4¼ x 1¼ in) for the borders on watercolour paper. Trace the egg on page 75 onto tracing paper with a soft pencil. Tape the tracing face down on the watercolour paper with masking tape. Redraw the egg to transfer it, then remove the tracing paper.

★★☆ **Skill level**   🕐 **3 hours**   **Techniques:** *Using templates p.11, Using a craft knife p. 11, Scoring p.11, Folding p.12*

3 Paint stripes on the strip and simple patterns on the egg with masking fluid using an artist's paintbrush. Leave to dry.

4 Resting on a sheet of scrap paper, use a flat paintbrush to paint the rectangle of watercolour paper yellow. (This is the card base). Thin the paint with water so brush strokes are visible in places. An even coverage is not necessary.

Helpful hint
When painting the watercolour paper, work quickly to give a free, loose effect.

5 Paint the strip pink and the egg with lilac, light blue and yellow paint. As before, thin the paints with water. When the paint has dried, gently rub off the masking fluid with your finger. Using a bone folder or craft knife, score across the centre of the card base, parallel with the short edges. Fold the card along the scored line.

Helpful hint
If you do not have a pair of fancy edged scissors, use pinking shears instead. Alternatively, cut a wavy edge with straight scissors.

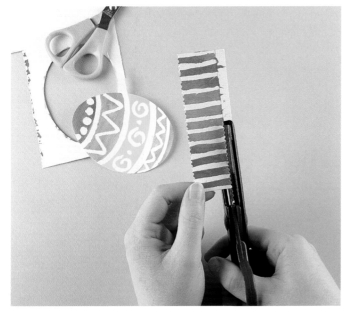

6 Resting on a cutting mat, cut across the ends of the pink and white strip. Cut out the egg with a craft knife. Cut just inside the long edges of the strip with a pair of fancy-edged scissors then cut the strip in half lengthwise.

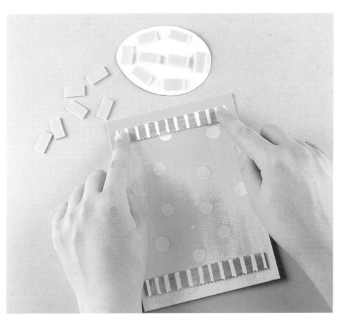

7 Stick pieces of adhesive foam to the reverse side of the strips and apply a double thick layer to the egg. Peel off the backing tapes. Stick the strips centrally 1 cm (½ in) in from the short edges of the card base. Stick the egg in the centre.

Embossed baby booties

Here is a charming greetings card to welcome a new baby. The pram and booties are embossed through a stencil to subtly create the motifs which are framed with fine foam. Bands of contrasting papers are embellished with cut-outs made with a paper punch.

Coloured writing paper is ideal to use for embossing. Choose paper that is 120gsm in weight.

You will need

Materials
- Tracing paper
- Stencil board
- Masking tape
- A5 sheet of light blue or pink writing paper
- A5 piece of fine yellow foam
- Spray adhesive
- A5 sheet of green paper
- A4 sheet of purple card

Tools
- Soft pencil
- Scissors
- Craft knife
- Metal ruler
- Cutting mat
- Ball embossing tool
- "Row of rectangles" paper punch
- Bone folder (optional)

1 Trace the templates on page 74 onto tracing paper with a soft pencil. Turn the tracing over and redraw the motifs on the reverse. Tape the tracing paper right side up on stencil board with masking tape. Transfer the motifs. Remove the tracing. Resting on a cutting mat, cut out the motifs with a craft knife.

2 Tape the stencil right side up on the right side of light blue or pink writing paper with masking tape. Turn the paper over.

★★☆ **Skill level**   🕐 **3 hours**   **Techniques:** *Using templates p. 11, Using a craft knife p. 11, Using spray adhesive p. 12*

3 Rub through the stencil with a ball embossing tool. The design will be embossed on the right side of the paper. Draw around the outer edge of the stencils. Remove the stencil. Cut along the drawn outer edges.

Helpful hint
A knitting needle or the rounded handle end of an artist's paint-brush can be used to emboss the motifs instead of an embossing tool.

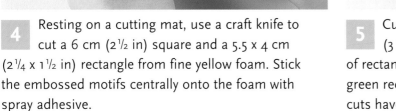

4 Resting on a cutting mat, use a craft knife to cut a 6 cm (2½ in) square and a 5.5 x 4 cm (2¼ x 1½ in) rectangle from fine yellow foam. Stick the embossed motifs centrally onto the foam with spray adhesive.

5 Cut an 8.5 x 7 cm (3½ x 2¾ in) and a 7.5 x 6.5 cm (3 x 2½ in) rectangle of green paper. Punch a row of rectangles centrally along one short edge of each green rectangle with a paper punch. Press hard so the cuts have neat edges.

6 Cut a 24 x 17 cm (9½ x 6¾ in) rectangle of purple card. Using a bone folder or craft knife, score across the centre parallel with the short edges. Fold the card in half along the scored line. Arrange the green paper rectangles on the card front. Position the foam on top. Stick all the pieces in place with spray adhesive.

Variation

Fancy pram

This three-dimensional greetings card has the embossed pram bordered by two layers of fine coloured foam, one of which has been cut with fancy-edge scissors.

Christmas handbag

These Christmas cards with a difference will add a surprise to the festive celebrations. The little bags of translucent paper contain a folded message and a scattering of Christmas sequins. Once the contents have been revealed, the handbags can be hung on the Christmas tree.

These pretty containers are also ideal for wedding and Valentine celebrations, simply add a suitable sequin motif, such as a heart.

You will need

Materials

- A5 sheet of coloured translucent paper
- Double-sided tape
- Tracing paper
- Scrap of thin card (optional)
- Gold glitter relief paint
- 30 cm (12 in) of fine gold cord
- Festive sequin shapes
- All-purpose household glue
- A5 sheet of gold paper

Tools

- Scissors
- Pencil
- Craft knife
- Metal ruler
- Cutting mat
- Bone folder (optional)
- Bradawl

1 Cut an 18 x 7.5 cm (7 x 3 in) rectangle of coloured translucent paper. Score across the centre parallel with the short edges and fold in half. Cut double-sided tape into two 8.5 cm (3¼ in) long, 5 mm (¼ in) wide strips and stick them along the long edges on one half. Fold down the other half to make the bag.

2 Trace the handbag template on page 75 onto tracing paper and cut it out. If you wish to make a number of handbags, cut the handbag from thin card to use as a durable template. Align the template and draw around the scallops on the handbag. Cut along the scallops.

★★☆ **Skill level**   🕐 **3 hours**   **Techniques:** *Using templates p. 11, Using a craft knife p. 11, Scoring p. 11, Folding p. 12*

3 Starting 2 cm (³/₄ in) below the upper edge, apply a row of dots just inside the long edges with gold glitter relief paint. Leave the glitter to dry.

Helpful hint
Loose glitter can be used instead of glitter relief paint. Dot PVA glue on the bag, sprinkle with loose glitter and shake off the excess.

4 Resting on a cutting mat, pierce a hole at the top corners of the bag with a bradawl. Thread the cord through the holes and knot the ends on the front. Cut off the excess cord.

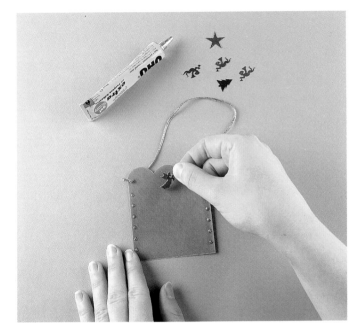

5 Glue a festive sequin to the front of the bag. Make sure that you apply the glue sparingly so it does not seep onto the paper. Alternatively, stick the sequin with a piece of double-sided tape.

6 Cut an 18 x 6 cm (7 x 2½ in) rectangle of gold paper. Write a message on the paper and fold it in half parallel with the short edges. Slip the message into the bag, folded edge first. Carefully pour some sequins inside the message.

Variation

Pink handbag

This pretty pink paper handbag is decorated with silver glitter and suspended on pink ribbon.

Driftwood ship

Here is a romantic sailing ship made from various recycled materials. The ship sails on a painted sea, its hull is a piece of driftwood and the sail is part of a map. With its travelling theme, this greetings card would make a delightful bon voyage card.

The cream background paper is subtly printed with white shells to echo the nautical theme.

You will need

Materials
- A3 sheet of cream patterned paper
- A3 sheet of cream card
- Spray adhesive
- Blue, aquamarine and cream acrylic paint
- Tracing paper
- Masking tape
- A5 piece of old map
- 12 cm (4³/₄ in) curved twig
- Scrap of fabric
- All-purpose household glue
- Piece of driftwood, approx. 11 x 5 cm (4¹/₂ x 2 in)

Tools
- Metal ruler
- Craft knife
- Cutting mat
- Bone folder (optional)
- Flat 2 cm (³/₄ in) paintbrush
- Soft pencil
- Scissors
- Hole punch

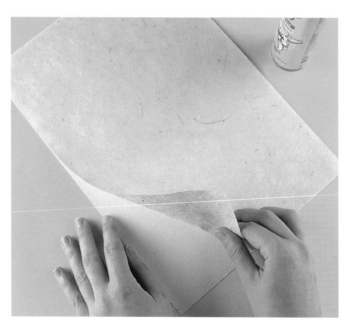

1 To strengthen the background paper, stick a 35 x 23 cm (14 x 9 in) rectangle of cream patterned paper and cream card together with spray adhesive. Cut out a 33 x 21.5 cm (13¹/₄ x 8¹/₂ in) rectangle. Score across the centre parallel with the short edges using a bone folder or craft knife. Fold along the scored line.

2 Mix together blue, aquamarine and cream acrylic paints. Pick up a little of the paint on a flat paintbrush. Paint across the lower 5.5 cm (2¹/₄ in) of the front of the card. Do not give an even coverage, allow the paper to show through in places. Leave to dry.

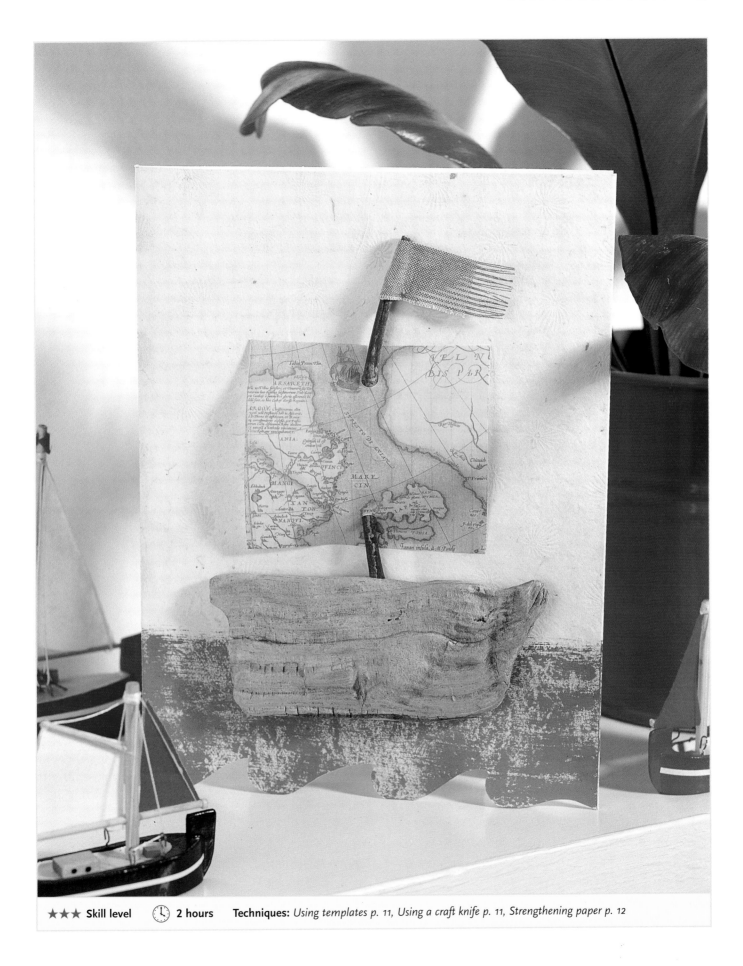

★★★ **Skill level**   🕐 **2 hours**   **Techniques:** *Using templates p. 11, Using a craft knife p. 11, Strengthening paper p. 12*

3 Trace the template on page 75 onto tracing paper with a soft pencil. Turn the tracing over and redraw the waves on the reverse side. Tape the tracing to the lower edge of the front of the card with masking tape. Redraw the waves on the lower edge to transfer them. Remove the tracing. Resting on a cutting mat, cut out the waves through both the front and back of the card using a craft knife.

4 Cut an 8.5 x 7.5 cm (3¼ x 3 in) rectangle from an old map for the sail. With a hole punch, make a hole in the centre of each of the long edges. Insert the twig, which will be the mast, through the punched holes.

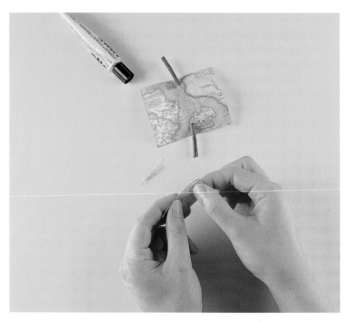

5 Cut a 5 x 2 cm (2 x ¾ in) rectangle from a scrap of fabric for the flag. Fray one short edge. Wrap the unfrayed edge of the flag around the top of the mast and glue it in place.

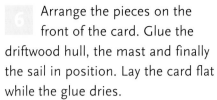

6 Arrange the pieces on the front of the card. Glue the driftwood hull, the mast and finally the sail in position. Lay the card flat while the glue dries.

Helpful hint
If you do not have a suitable piece of driftwood, cut a hull from balsa wood using a craft knife.

Variation

Little boat

This driftwood boat has two metal eyelets screwed into the top of its driftwood hull. A hole has been pierced in the centre with a bradawl and a twig mast inserted. Fine string is tied to the eyelets and bound around the top of the twig. A fabric flag tops the mast and the boat is glued to blue cloud-effect paper applied to a turquoise blue card base.

Pressed flower trellis

Gather pretty flowers from the garden to make this beautiful greetings card which is ideal for a nature lover. The trellis effect is made from pressed lavender sprigs and stems fastened with raffia. The trellis then frames a set of colourful pressed flowers. Applying the design to handmade paper embedded with petals emphasizes the floral theme.

Pressed leaves would make a charming alternative to flowers. Choose foliage in rich autumnal shades for a birthday later in the year. Press stems with a small leaf at the tip for the uprights of the trellis.

You will need

Materials

- Fresh flowers including lavender sprigs
- Blotting paper
- A3 sheet of thick handmade paper embedded with petals
- PVA glue
- Raffia

Tools

- Flower press (or heavy book)
- Metal ruler
- Fine artist's paintbrush
- Bone folder or craft knife
- Glue spreader
- Scissors
- Large-eyed needle
- Tweezers

1 Pick flower heads no wider than 3 cm (1¼ in) and lavender sprigs, picking more than you need in case they break or the petals crease. Carefully place the flowers between layers of blotting paper and press flat in a flower press for about one week. Gently peel back the papers to reveal the pressed flowers.

2 To tear a deckle-effect edge, place a ruler on thick handmade paper. Moisten a fine artist's paintbrush and run it along the paper against the ruler to weaken the paper. Tear the paper against the ruler to make two 15 cm (6 in) squares for the front and back of the card.

★★★ **Skill level**   🕐 **3 hours**   **Techniques:** *Scoring p. 11, Tearing a deckle edge p. 12*

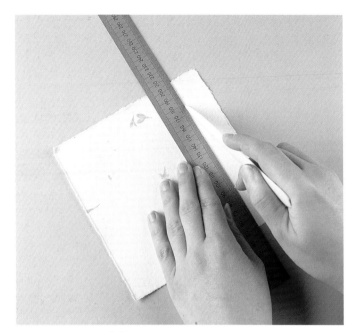

3 On one of the squares, score a margin 3 cm (1 1/4 in) in from the left-hand edge with a bone folder or craft knife to make a hinge. Bend the hinge forwards. This is the front of the card.

4 Arrange three pressed lavender sprigs upright on the card front 4 cm (1 1/2 in) apart and 1 cm (1/2 in) below the top edge. Glue the heads in place.

5 Cut the heads off another three lavender sprigs. Lay one stem horizontally across the upright sprigs below the heads. Thread the needle with raffia and bring it from the back to the right side and sew a cross over the sprigs at the two outer intersections to secure. Tie the raffia ends together on the underside.

6 Lay the remaining stems across the uprights 4 cm (1 1/2 in) apart forming a trellis and sew in place as before. Trim the sprigs to 1 cm (1/2 in) beyond the trellis.

7 Use a pair of tweezers to gently lift the flowers from the blotting paper. Use a glue spreader to spread PVA glue sparingly on the flower heads and stick a flower within each trellis square.

8 Glue a pressed lavender sprig on the hinge. Place the card front onto the back. Sew the sprig in place through both card layers with raffia in a cross stitch at the top and bottom of the stem, tying the ends securely on the back. Cut off the excess raffia.

Variation

Bunch of flowers

Bunch together a group of pressed lavender sprigs on the front of a folded rectangle of handmade paper embedded with petals and leaves. Stick the arrangement in place with PVA glue. Thread a large-eyed needle with fine silk ribbon and bind it a few times around the stems by sewing through the card. Tie the ribbon on the front of the card.

Rubber-stamped Dutch scene

Creating designs with a rubber stamp is a great way to get professional results very quickly. This greetings card features a stamped picture of a tranquil Dutch scene embellished with scraps of lace, ribbon and buttons. The back of the greetings card extends beyond the front opening edge and has a decorative border that is still visible when the recipient opens the card to read it.

This is a great way to use up scraps of lace, ribbon and buttons as only small quantities are needed.

You will need

Materials

- Blue ink pad
- A4 sheet of white card
- A3 sheet of cream ridged card
- Spray adhesive
- Scraps of edging lace
- 1 cm (½ in) wide blue gingham ribbon
- Red stranded cotton embroidery thread
- 4 red buttons
- All-purpose household glue

Tools

- Windmill rubber stamp
- Craft knife
- Cutting mat
- Metal ruler
- Bone folder (optional)
- Needlework scissors
- Large crewel embroidery needle

1 Gently press the rubber stamp onto the ink pad, make sure you cover the entire stamp with ink. Stamp the picture onto white card and allow to dry. Using a craft knife on a cutting mat, cut out leaving a 1 cm (½ in) border around the stamped picture. Measure the picture including the border.

2 Cut a strip of cream, ridged card that is the height of the picture plus 3 cm (1¼ in), and twice its width plus 9 cm (3½ in). Measure along one long edge of the card the width of the picture plus 6 cm (2½ in). Use a bone folder to score across the card at this point. Fold. Stick the picture to the front with spray adhesive.

★★★ **Skill level**   🕐 **2 hours**   **Techniques:** *Scoring p. 11, Using spray adhesive p. 12*

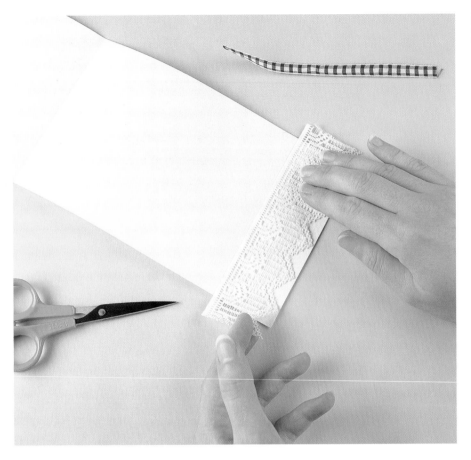

3 Use spray adhesive to stick wide lace to the inside of the card along the extending right-hand edge. Stick a length of gingham ribbon on top. Cut the ends of the lace and ribbon level with the card.

4 Using spray adhesive stick narrow lace each side of the picture parallel with the short edges. Cut the ends of the lace level with the card with scissors.

5 Thread a large crewel embroidery needle with six strands of red stranded cotton embroidery thread. Sew along the two narrow strips of edging lace with a running stitch, fastening the ends of the thread on the underside of the card. Cut off the excess thread.

6 As a finishing touch, glue a red button to each corner of the picture with all-purpose household glue.

Helpful hint
To emboss the stamped picture, sprinkle embossing powder on the design whilst the ink is still wet. Shake off the excess powder. Carefully fix the powder using a precision heat tool.

Wire dragonfly

This elegant dragonfly is modelled from coloured wire and its wings accentuated with translucent paper. Vibrant coloured wires in various thicknesses are now available from craft shops and specialist suppliers. They bend easily and are ideal for craft work. The dragonfly is applied to a background of white paper embedded with colourful fibres then framed with a bold, metallic turquoise card.

Modelling the dragonfly with wire allows the design to be gently manipulated to create a realistic pose.

You will need

Materials

- 1 mm ($\frac{1}{24}$ in) diameter green wire
- 0.5 mm ($\frac{1}{48}$ in) diameter green wire
- Spray adhesive
- A5 sheet of translucent green paper
- A4 sheet of white decorative paper
- A4 sheet of white card
- Clear adhesive tape
- A3 sheet of turquoise metallic card
- Double-sided tape

Tools

- Wire cutters or an old pair of scissors
- Scissors
- Craft knife
- Metal ruler
- Cutting mat
- Fine artist's paintbrush
- Large needle
- Bone folder (optional)

1 Snip four 19 cm (7½ in) lengths of 1 mm (¼₄ in) diameter wire for the wings with wire cutters or an old pair of scissors. Bend each length into a loop, overlapping the ends by 2 cm (³⁄₄ in). Twist a length of 0.5 mm (¹⁄₄₈ in) diameter wire around the crossover of the thicker wire a few times to secure in place.

2 Spray the wings with spray adhesive and press them onto translucent green paper. Cut away the excess paper around the wings with a pair of scissors.

★★★ **Skill level**   🕐 **2 hours**   **Techniques:** *Scoring p. 11, Using spray adhesive p. 12, Strengthening paper p. 12*

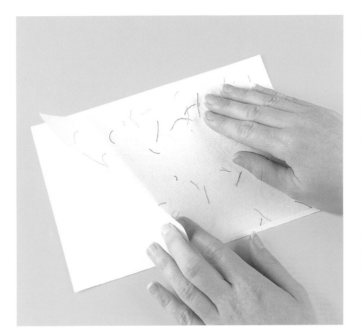

3 Apply a 21 x 14 cm (8¼ x 5½ in) rectangle of white decorative paper to white card with spray adhesive to stiffen it. Cut down to a 19 x 12 cm (7½ x 4¾ in) rectangle with a craft knife against a metal ruler, resting on a cutting mat.

4 Cut a 1 cm (½ in) slit centrally, 4 cm (1½ in) down from the top of the stiffened paper, with a craft knife. Push the scissor blades through the slit to widen it enough to insert the wires through.

5 Bend the extending ends of the wing wires downwards at right angles and insert through the slit. Arrange the wings in pairs each side of the slit. Bend back the wire ends under the stiffened paper and splay them open. Stick pieces of clear adhesive tape over the wire ends to hold them in place.

Helpful hint
The translucent paper used for the wings is a delicate, figured Japanese paper. Plain, coloured tissue paper is an inexpensive but satisfactory alternative.

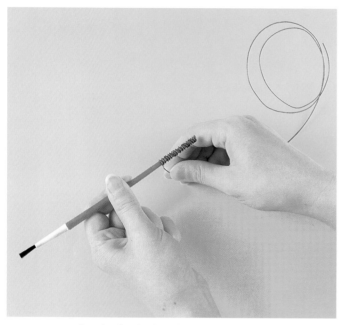

6   To make the body, bind 1 mm (¹/₂₄ in) diameter wire tightly around a fine artist's paintbrush starting at the top of the handle end. Continue binding until the coiled body is about 8 cm (3¹/₄ in) long. Slip the body off the paintbrush. Snip off the excess wire. Position the body over the wings.

7   With a large needle, pierce a hole in the paper under the centre of the body and another hole 1.5 cm (³/₄ in) below the first. Thread 0.5 mm (¹/₄₈ in) diameter wire up through one hole, then between a few coils of the body, back through the other hole and twist the ends together to hold the body to the paper.

8   Cut a 32 x 23 cm (12¹/₂ x 9 in) rectangle of turquoise metallic card. Using a bone folder or craft knife, score across the centre parallel with the short edges. Fold the card in half along the scored line. Apply double-sided tape to the edges of the stiffened paper on the reverse side. Peel off the backing tapes and stick to the front of the card. Bend the body at a jaunty angle and curve the centre of the wings upwards.

Pricked and stitched seed-head

Making greetings cards and embroidery are the most popular of crafts. You can combine these mediums to make a pretty card using simple stitches on paper. The design is first pricked with a pin to provide a guide for the embroidery, which is worked with vibrant blue thread.

Coton perle embroidery thread comes in lots of bright colours. Choose a shade that really stands out against your background paper.

You will need

Materials

- A4 sheet of pale orange mottled paper
- A4 sheet of cream card
- Spray adhesive
- Tracing paper
- Masking tape
- Blue coton perle embroidery thread
- A4 sheet of silver card

Tools

- Scissors
- Soft pencil
- Cutting mat
- Glass-headed pin
- Crewel embroidery needle
- Craft knife
- Metal ruler
- Bone folder (optional)

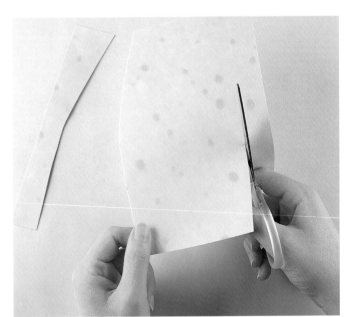

1 To strengthen the background paper, stick a 20 x 15 cm (8 x 6 in) rectangle of pale orange mottled paper and cream card together with spray adhesive. Cut out an 18.5 x 11 cm (7¼ x 4¼ in) rectangle with a pair of scissors. Shape one of the long sides.

2 Trace the seed-head template on page 75 onto tracing paper with a soft pencil. Tape the tracing to the background paper with masking tape. Resting on a cutting mat, prick a hole at each dot with a glass-headed pin. Remove the tracing.

★★★ **Skill level**   ⏱ **4 hours**   **Techniques:** *Using templates p. 11, Using spray adhesive p. 12, Strengthening paper p. 12*

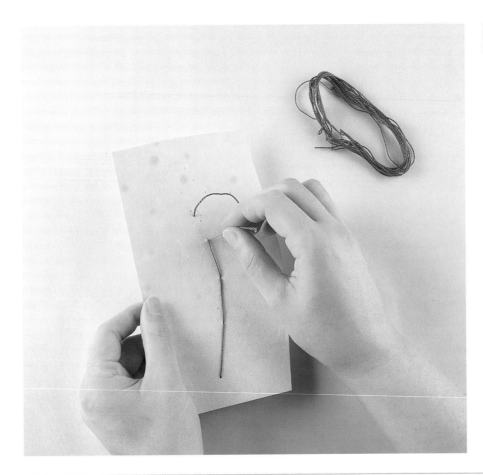

3 Thread the needle with a length of embroidery thread. Knot the end. To work the stem in backstitch, bring the needle to the right side through the second hole from the bottom. Insert the needle through the lowest hole and up through the third hole, pulling the thread to lay smoothly on the paper. Continue to the top of the stem at the centre of the seed-head.

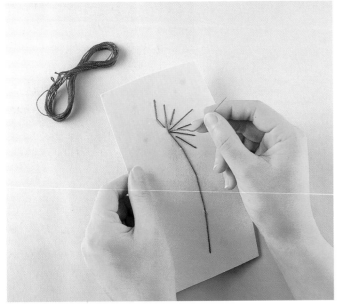

4 Now work the seed-head in straight stitches, radiating out from the top of the stem.

5 Place the background paper on the cutting mat and pierce four holes with the pin around the end of each straight stitch for the seeds which will be worked in French knots.

6 Knot the thread end and bring it to the right side through a pierced hole. Twist the thread twice around the needle then insert the needle back through the hole and pull the thread tight. Repeat on all the holes.

7 Cut a 26 x 21 cm (10½ x 8¼ in) rectangle of silver card. Using a bone folder or craft knife, score across the centre parallel with the short edges. Fold the card in half along the scored line. Stick the seed head centrally to the front of the card with spray adhesive.

Helpful hint
Choose a glass-headed pin instead of an ordinary dressmaking pin to prick the design as it is much kinder to your fingers.

Stencilled Oriental screen

The chrysanthemum is often to be found decorating the beautiful screens and embroideries of the Far East. Recreate your own miniature Oriental screen by stencilling a triptych card with trailing pink chrysanthemums. As a pretty finishing touch, the stencilled flowers are highlighted with gold relief paint.

The chrysanthemum is the national flower of Japan and symbolizes purity and longevity.

You will need

Materials

- Tracing paper
- Stencil board, 25.5 x 16.5 cm (10 x 6½ in)
- Masking tape
- A4 sheet of gold and cream marbled paper
- Mid-pink and deep pink acrylic paints
- Kitchen towel
- A4 sheet of purple card
- Spray adhesive
- Gold relief paint

Tools

- Soft pencil
- Scissors
- Cutting mat
- Craft knife
- Metal ruler
- 2 cm (³⁄₄ in) and 1 cm (½ in) stencil brushes
- Bone folder (optional)

1 Trace the screen template on page 76 with a soft pencil onto tracing paper. Turn the paper over and redraw it on the reverse side. Tape the tracing, right side up, onto the stencil board with masking tape. Redraw to transfer the design. Remove the tracing. Resting on a cutting mat, cut out the stencil with a craft knife.

2 Tape the stencil right side up on the marbled paper with masking tape. Pick up a little mid-pink paint on the 2 cm (³⁄₄ in) stencil brush. Dab off the excess on a kitchen towel. Holding the brush upright, dab the paint through the stencils. Clean the brush.

★★★ **Skill level**   ⏱ **4 hours**   **Techniques:** *Using templates p. 11, Using a craft knife p. 11, Using spray adhesive p. 12*

3 Allow the paint to dry. Pick up a little deep pink paint on the 1 cm (½ in) stencil brush, dabbing off the excess on a kitchen towel. Holding the brush upright, dab the paint in the centre of each full flower and at the base of each quarter flower to shade them. Clean the brush and leave the paint to dry.

Helpful hint
If you cannot find gold and cream marbled paper, create a similar effect by sponging gold paint randomly onto cream paper with a natural sponge.

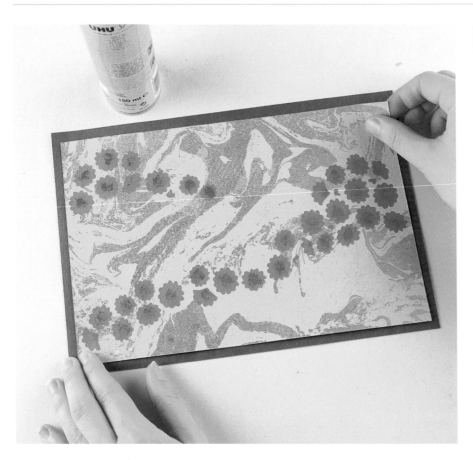

4 Draw around the edges of the stencil on the marble paper then cut out the rectangle. Cut a 27 x 18 cm (10½ x 7 in) rectangle of purple card. Stick the stencilled paper centrally onto the card with spray adhesive, smoothing the paper outwards.

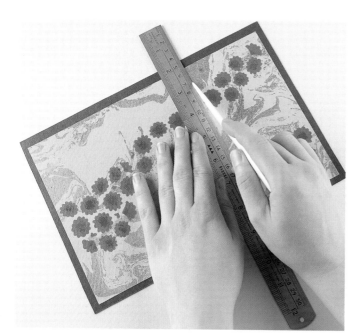

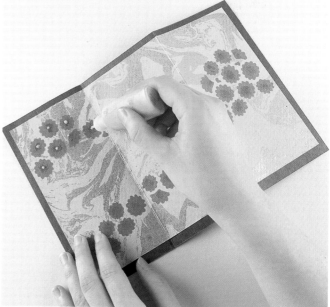

5 Using a bone folder or craft knife, score across the screen 9 cm (3 ½ in) in from both of the short edges of the purple card. Fold the card in concertina folds along the two scored lines.

6 Open the card out flat and dot gold relief paint in the centre of each full flower and at the base of each quarter flower. Leave to dry then refold the card along the scored lines.

Variation

Pink flowers

This single fold greetings card has one third of the stencil worked with white acrylic paint onto colourful paper and applied to a folded pink card. The flowers are blushed with pale pink and highlighted with a bright pink relief paint.

Glass-painted sun-catcher

Glass paints applied to acetate give the effect of translucent stained glass. This exotic greetings card can also be given as a gift as the glass painted design, inspired by Moorish tiles, is attached with a brass paper fastener and can be removed to suspend by a window where it will catch the sunlight.

Glass paints are easy to apply. The colour is flooded into the reservoirs that have been created with glass painting outliner.

You will need

Materials
- Tracing paper
- Clear acetate
- Masking tape
- Gold glass painting outliner
- White paper
- Scissors
- Pale blue, green and deep blue glass paints
- A3 sheet of white card
- Brass paper fastener

Tools
- Black pen
- Soft pencil
- Artist's paintbrush
- Cutting mat
- Craft knife
- Metal ruler
- Bradawl
- Bone folder (optional)

1 Trace the card front on page 77 onto tracing paper with a black pen. Redraw the peaks along the upper edge on the reverse side with a soft pencil. Tape the acetate over the tracing paper with masking tape. Trace the design onto the acetate with gold glass painting outliner. Allow to dry.

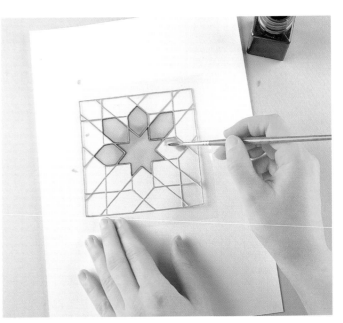

2 Rest the acetate on white paper so the painted areas will show clearly. Paint the central star areas pale blue. To paint each reservoir, load an artist's paintbrush with paint and place it in the centre of the reservoir to fill the area with colour. Brush the paint into the corners and up to the outliner.

★★★ **Skill level**   ⏱ **4 hours**   **Techniques:** *Using templates p. 11, Using a craft knife p. 11, Scoring p. 11, Folding p. 12*

3 Paint the small triangles surrounding the star green and the border deep blue. Leave the paints to dry overnight.

Helpful hint

If you have not painted up to the outliner in places, do not apply more paint as this will create an unattractive line of colour. Instead, thicken the line with more outliner.

4 Cut out the sun-catcher. Resting on a cutting mat, pierce a hole at the dot (refer to the tracing) with a bradawl. This is where the brass paper fastener will be positioned.

5 Cut a 30.5 x 21.5 cm (12 x 8½ in) rectangle of white card. Using a bone folder or craft knife, score across the centre of the card parallel with the short edges. Fold the card in half along the scored line. Tape the tracing to the front of the card with masking tape. Redraw the upper edge to transfer the peaks, also transfer the dot. Remove the tracing.

6 Resting on a cutting mat, cut out the peaks through both thicknesses of the card with a craft knife. Open the card out flat. Resting on the cutting mat, pierce a hole at the dot with a bradawl.

7 Insert a brass paper fastener through the hole on the sun-catcher, then through the hole on the card front. Splay open the prongs inside the card to secure the sun-catcher in place.

Silk-painted paisley series

It is sometimes useful to produce a series of greetings cards — for invitations, announcements or Christmas cards, for example. These silk-painted cards look very special but it is actually quick to produce a number at a time. For a quirky touch, the designs are applied to triangular cards — a great way to use up scraps of coloured card.

Apply white paper behind the silk if the motif is to be applied to coloured card to prevent the card showing through the fine fabric.

You will need

Materials

- 30 cm (12 in) square of white habutai silk
- Tracing paper
- Masking tape
- Gold silk outliner (gutta)
- Blue, green, purple and deep yellow silk paints
- 2 sheets of white tissue paper
- White paper
- Spray adhesive
- A4 sheets of coloured card

Tools

- Iron
- Soft pencil
- Scissors
- 30 cm (12 in) silk frame
- 3-point silk pins
- Artist's paintbrush
- Cutting mat
- Craft knife
- Metal ruler
- Bone folder (optional)

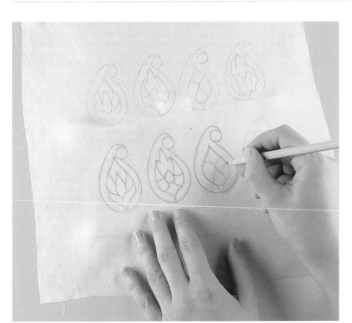

1 Press the silk. Trace the paisley templates on page 77 onto tracing paper. Tape the silk on top with masking tape and trace a row of paisley motifs with a soft pencil. Remove the tracing then replace it to trace another row of motifs below the first.

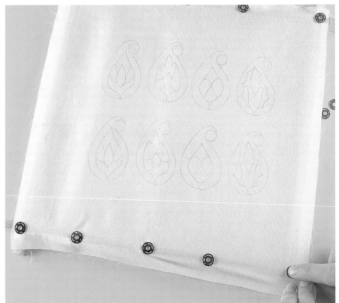

2 Lay the silk centrally on the silk frame. Starting at the middle of one edge, pin the silk smoothly to the frame with 3-point silk pins. Repeat on the opposite edge of the frame and then the other two edges smoothing the silk outwards towards the corners so that it lays smooth and taut.

★★★ **Skill level**   🕐 **4 hours**   **Techniques:** *Using templates p. 11, Using a craft knife p. 11, Using spray adhesive p. 12*

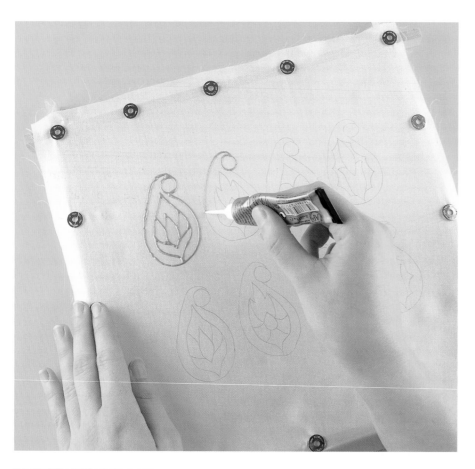

3 Redraw the rows of paisley motifs on the silk with gold silk outliner (gutta). Leave to dry.

Helpful hint

Before painting, check to see if any outliner (gutta) lines do not join up or are very thin. If this is the case go over them again to fill any gaps so the paint cannot seep into the other sections.

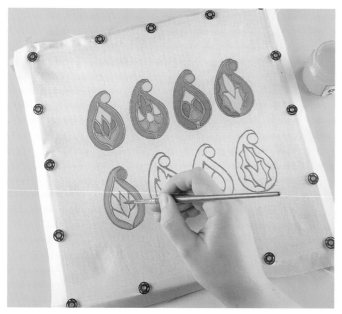

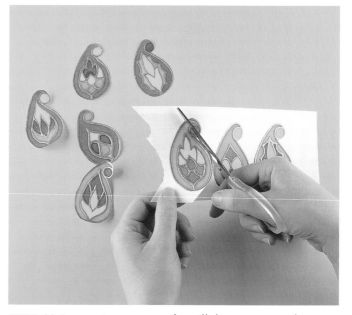

4 Dip the paintbrush into one of the silk paints. Press the brush onto the centre of one of the areas, the paint will flow up to the outline. Paint all of the paisley motifs, cleaning the paintbrush with water when changing colours. Set aside to dry.

5 Using an iron, press the silk between two layers of white tissue paper to fix the paints. Roughly cut out the two rows of paisley motifs. Stick the rows to white paper with spray adhesive, smoothing the silk outwards to eliminate air bubbles. Cut out each motif with a pair of scissors.

6 Trace the triangle template on page 77 onto tracing paper with a soft pencil. Turn the tracing paper over and redraw the triangle on the reverse side. Tape the tracing paper right side up onto one of the coloured cards with masking tape. Redraw the triangle to transfer it. Repeat to draw eight triangles on the various colours. Resting on a cutting mat and using a metal ruler, cut out the triangles with a craft knife. Score across the centre of the triangle using a bone folder or craft knife.

7 Fold the card in half along the scored line. Stick a paisley motif to the front of each triangle with spray adhesive.

FOLESHILL

Templates

Templates shown are not full size. Set photocopier
to 118% to copy to correct size for projects.

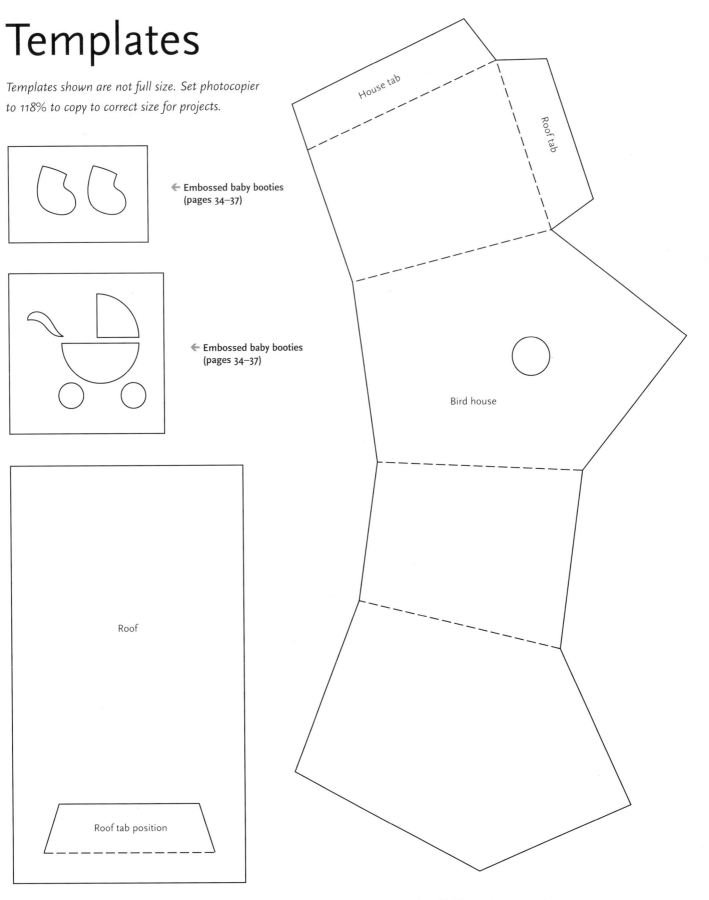

← Embossed baby booties
(pages 34–37)

← Embossed baby booties
(pages 34–37)

House tab

Roof tab

Bird house

Roof

Roof tab position

↑ 3D bird house (pages 14–17)

↑ 3D bird house (pages 14–17)

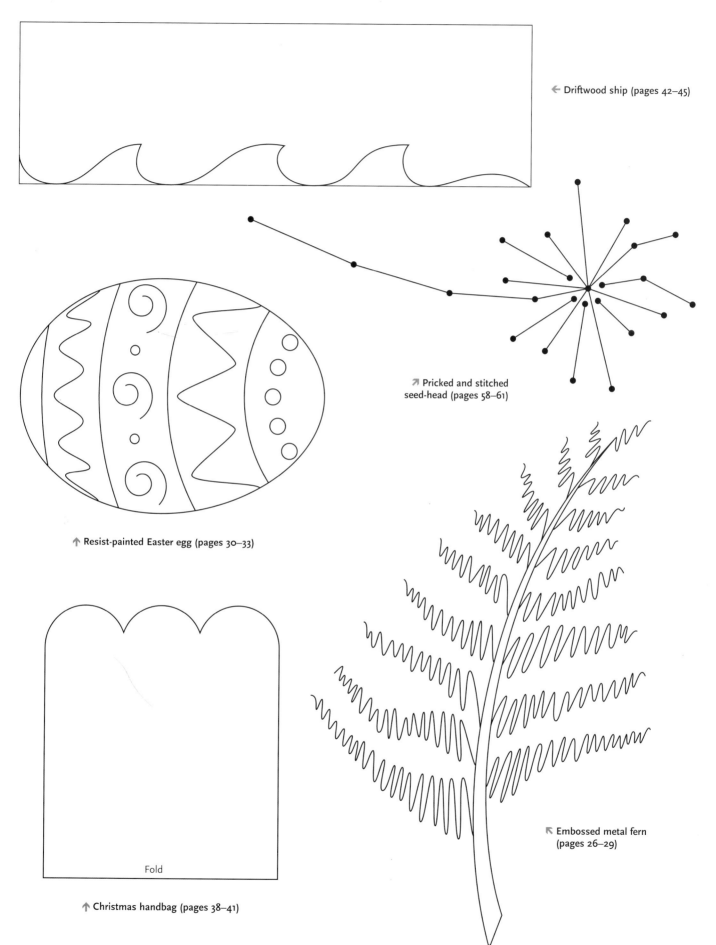

← Driftwood ship (pages 42–45)

↗ Pricked and stitched
seed-head (pages 58–61)

↑ Resist-painted Easter egg (pages 30–33)

↖ Embossed metal fern
(pages 26–29)

Fold

↑ Christmas handbag (pages 38–41)

Templates shown are not full size. Set photocopier to 118% to copy to correct size for projects.

↑ **Stencilled Oriental screen (pages 62–65)**

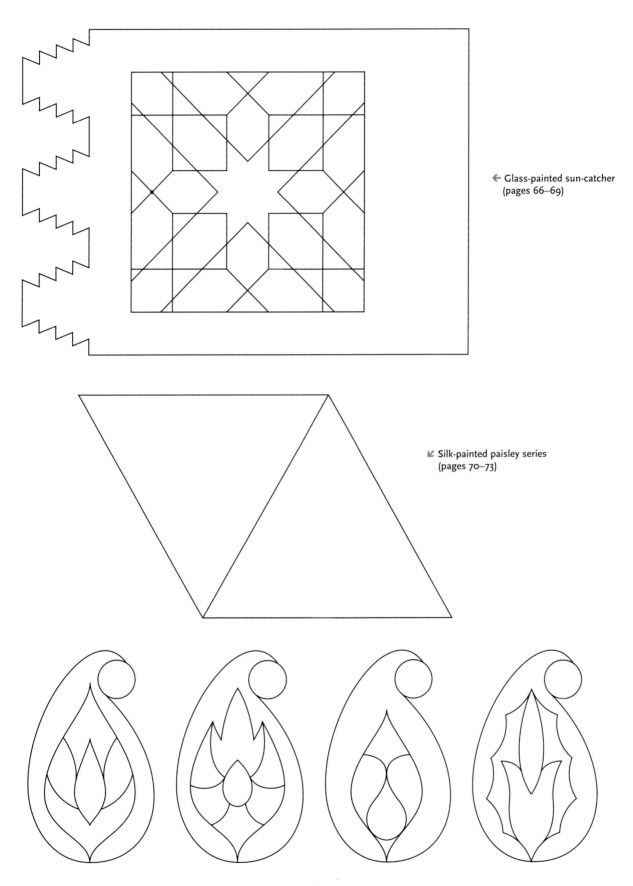

← Glass-painted sun-catcher
(pages 66–69)

↙ Silk-painted paisley series
(pages 70–73)

↑ Silk-painted paisley series (pages 70–73)

Suppliers

UNITED KINGDOM

L. Cornelissen & Son Ltd
105 Great Russell Street
London WC1B 3RY
Tel: 020 7636 1045
Also:
1A Hercules Street
London N7 6AT
Tel: 020 7281 8870
General craft supplier.

Cowling & Wilcox
26–28 Broadwick Street
London W1F 8HX
Tel: 020 7734 9557
www.cowlingandwilcox.com
Email: art@cowlingandwilcox.com
General craft supplier.

Craft Creations
Ingersoll House
Delamare Road
Cheshunt
Hertfordshire EN8 9ND
Tel: 01992 781 900
Email: enquiries@craftcreations.com
www.craftcreations.com
General craft supplier.

Cranberry Card Company
Unit 4 Greenway Workshops
Bedwas House Ind. Est.
Bedwas
Caephilly CF83 8DW
Tel: 02920 807941
www.cranberrycards.co.uk
Email: info@cranberrycards.co.uk
www.cranberrycards.co.uk
Selection of card, paper and accessories.

The English Stamp Company
Worth Matravers
Dorset BH19 3JP
Tel: 01929 439 117

Email: sales@englishstamp.com
www.englishstamp.com
Suppliers of stamps, paints, inkpads and handmade paper. Mail-order only.

Falkiner Fine Papers Ltd
76 Southampton Row
London WC1B 4AR
Tel: 020 7831 1151
Carries a large range of handmade papers. Also offers a mail-order service.

Homecrafts Direct
Unit 2, Wanlip Rd Syston
Leicester
LE7 1PD
Tel: 0116 269 7733
www.homecrafts.co.uk
Email: info@homecrafts.co.uk
Mail-order service. Selection of handmade papers and range of craft products.

Paperchase
Flagship Store and Main Office
213 Tottenham Court Road
London W1T 7PS
Tel: 020 7467 6200
Retailers of stationery, wrapping paper and art materials. Call for your nearest outlet.

Mail order service
Tel: 0161 839 1500
www.paperchase.co.uk
Email: mailorder@paperchase.co.uk

T N Lawrence
208 Portland Rd
Hove
East Sussex BN3 5QT
Tel: 01273 260260
www.lawrence.co.uk
Carries a large range of papers as well as general artist's materials.

The Stencil Store
41A Heronsgate Road
Chorleywood
Herts WD3 5BL
Tel: 01923 285577
Email: stencilstore@onetel.com
www.stencilstore.com
Supply wide range of stencil designs. Phone for nearest store or to order catalogue.

AUSTRALIA

Artwise Amazing Paper
186 Enmore Road
Enmore, NSW 2042
Tel: 02 9519 8237
www.amazingpaper.com.au

Lincraft
www.lincraft.com.au
General craft supplier. Stores throughout Australia

Myer Centre, Rundle Mall
Adelaide, SA 5000
Tel: 02 8231 6611

Myer Centre, Queen Street
Brisbane, QLD 4000
Tel: 07 3221 0064

Shop D02/D03
Canberra Centre, Bunda Street
Canberra, ACT 2601
Tel: 02 6257 4516

Australia on Collins
Melbourne, VIC 3000
Tel: 03 9650 1609

Imperial Arcade, Pitt Street
Sydney, NSW 2000
Tel: 02 9221 5111

Paper Fantasy
256a Charters Towers Road
Hermit Park, QLD 4812
Tel: 07 4725 1272

Paperwright
124 Lygon Street
Carlton, VIC 3053
Tel: 03 9663 8747

Spotlight
Tel: 1800 656 256
www.spotlight.com.au
*General craft supplier. Call for nearest
store.*

SOUTH AFRICA

Art Shop
140A Victoria Avenue
Benoni West 1503
Tel/Fax: 011 421 1030

Arts, Crafts and Hobbies
72 Hibernia Street
George 6529
Tel/Fax: 044 874 1337
Mail-order service available.

Pen and Art
Shop 313, Musgrave Centre
Musgrave Road
Durban 4001
Tel/Fax: 031 201 0094

Bowker Arts and Crafts
52 4th Avenue
Newton Park
Port Elizabeth 6001
Tel: 041 365 2487
Fax: 041 365 5306

Centurion Kuns
Shop 45, Eldoraigne Shopping Mall
Saxby Road
Eldoraigne
0157
Tel/Fax: 012 654 0449

Crafty Supplies
Shop UG 2, Stadium on Main
Main Road, Claremont 7700
Cape Town
Tel: 021 671 0286
Fax: 021 671 0308

Creative Papercraft
64 Judd Street
Horizon
1724
Tel/Fax: 011 763 5682

L & P Stationery and Art
141 Zastron Street
Westdene
Bloemfontein 9301
Tel: 051 430 1085
Fax: 051 430 4102

Le Papier du Port
Gardens Centre
Cape Town 8000
Tel: 021 462 4796
Fax: 021 461 9281
Mail-order service available.

Scarab Paper
Next to Engen Garage on the N2
  between Sedgefield and George
Tel: 044 343 2455
Fax: 044 343 1828
E-mail: scarabpaper@mweb.co.za

NEW ZEALAND

Brush & Palette
50 Lichfield Street
Christchurch
Tel/Fax: 03 366 3088

Fine Art Papers
200 Madras Street
Christchurch
Tel: 03 379 4410
Fax: 03 379 4443

Gordon Harris Art Supplies
4 Gillies Ave
Newmarket
Auckland
Tel: 09 520 4466
Fax: 09 520 0880
and
31 Symonds St
Auckland Central
Tel: 09 377 9992

Littlejohns
170 Victoria Street
Wellington
Tel: 04 385 2099
Fax: 04 385 2090

Studio Art Supplies
81 Parnell Rise
Parnell
Auckland
Tel: 09 377 0302
Fax: 09 377 7657

G Webster & Co Ltd
44 Manners Street
Wellington
Tel: 04 384 2134
Fax: 04 384 2968

Index